# AROUND the WORLD with

# 30 PASTRIES

## Easy Home-Style Recipes

**William David Welch**

# PASTRIES

## From around the

# World

# Contents

**RECIPE**

# German Franzbrötchen

Ready in **20 minutes**

Serves **8 people**

**280 calories** per serving

### History

Franzbrötchen stems from Hamburg in Germany and was believed to have been brought to Hamburg by Napoleon's troops during the occupation. A variation on a cinnamon bun this pastry is delightfully sweet and tasty.

**Ingredients**

Dough:

- 4 cups of flour
- ¾ cup + 1 ½ tablespoon milk, lukewarm
- 1 packet dry yeast
- 1 cup of sugar
- ½ cup of butter
- 1 egg
- Pinch of salt
- Pepper

Filling:

- ½ cup of butter (melted)
- ½ cup of sugar
- 1 tablespoon of cinnamon

**Preparation**

1. Spoon flour onto a clean counter and form a small hole. Add a touch of the lukewarm milk, then the yeast. Add a bit of sugar. Gently stir with your fingers for 3-5 minutes.
2. Add the remainder of the milk and the sugar. Add the egg, butter, salt, and pepper. Press everything into soft, smooth dough. Leave the dough to rest in a warmish spot for 30 minutes.
3. Using a rolling pin, roll the dough out into a rectangle about a ¼ inch thick.
4. Wash with the melted butter and sprinkle with the mixed cinnamon and sugar. Roll the dough into a roll, and cut into pieces about 2 inches thick. Place on a baking sheet and use the end of a wooden spoon to gently press down on the middle of each piece.
5. Brush with more melted butter, and bake at 340 degrees F for about 15 minutes until golden brown.

**Tips**

Make sure you leave enough space between the pastries on the baking tray as they will expand in the oven.

**Tools**

Rolling pin, mixing bowl, baking tray, sharp knife, measuring cup

# Indian Gulab Jamun

Ready in **40 minutes**

Serves **24-30 people**

**125 calories** per serving

### History

Gulab Jamun is known as the Indian doughnut. It is a delicious sweet treat which is made and enjoyed by Indians across the globe. The original recipe is believed to have come from Persia, however the Gulab Jamun have since been adapted to become known as the Indian doughnut

### Ingredients

Batter:

- 1 cup of flour plus an additional ¼ cup flour for dusting (cake flour)
- 1 tablespoon of butter
- 1 tablespoon of semolina
- 1 teaspoon of baking powder
- ½ teaspoon bicarbonate of soda
- ½ teaspoon of powdered cardamom
- ½ a tin of condensed milk
- 1 cup of vegetable oil

Syrup:

- 1 cup of white sugar
- 1 ½ cups of water
- 1 tablespoon of rose water

**Preparation**

1. Combine the dry ingredients together (remember to only use a cup of flour). Then add the butter and work it into the mixture to form a crumb-like texture.
2. Mix in the condensed milk until you have a soft dough. Then work in the additional ¼ cup flour so that you are left with stiff dough. Leave to rest.
3. To make the syrup add the sugar to a medium-sized pot and add the water. Boil together remembering to stir continuously. Once the sugar has dissolved allow the mixture to thicken slightly. Take the pot off the heat before the syrup gets too thick.
4. Now it's time to shape your dough. Roll the dough into long fingers. The batter will expand when it is fried.
5. Use a heavy- bottomed pan to bring the oil up to a medium heat. Place the batter fingers into the pan and fry until golden brown..
6. Take the Gulab Jamuns out of the oil and place them in the syrup mixture.
7. The Gulab Jamun can be served hot or cold.

**Tips**

To make coconut Gulab Jamun you will need 2 cups of desiccated coconut (after dipping in the syrup dip into the coconut)

You can use ghee instead of butter for a more authentically Indian recipe.

**Tools**

Mixing bowl, medium-sized pot, heavy-bottomed pan, stovetop, airtight container, baking rack

# Portuguese Pasteis de Nata

Ready in **2hr 35minutes**

Serves **12 people**

**210 calories** per serving

## History

Also known as Portuguese Custard Tarts, Pasteis de Nata had its roots in the Jerónimos Monastery where it is believed to have been created. The recipe dates back as far as the 18th century. During this time, the monks used the whites of eggs to starch their clothing and so they needed a way to make use of the egg yolks. Thus the Pasteis de Nata was born.

## Ingredients

Dough:

- 1 cup of flour (all-purpose)
- ¼ teaspoon salt
- ⅓ cup of cold water
- 8 tablespoons of butter (unsalted and softened)

Sugar Syrup:

- ¾ cup of white sugar
- ¼ cup of water (plus an additional tablespoon of water)
- 1 stick of cinnamon (optional)
- 1 lemon (zested into broad strips) (optional)

Custard Base:

- ⅓ cup of flour (all-purpose)
- ¼ teaspoon of salt
- 1½ cups of milk (room temperature)
- 6 large eggs (only the yolks are needed)
- 1 teaspoon of vanilla extract (optional)

**Preparation**

1. In a large mixing bowl, add the flour, salt, and cold water. Combine by mixing with a wooden spoon. Mix until the dough begins to come together to form a sticky mixture..
2. Place the formed dough onto a flour-covered countertop. Sprinkle some additional flour over the ball of dough to make it more workable. Knead for two minutes and then cover and leave for 20 minutes.
3. After the rest period is over, roll the dough into a square. You want it to be about ½-inch in thickness. Dust lightly with flour again making sure the dough is still sticky.
4. Using a silicone spatula, spread ⅓ of the softened butter over the square. Leave a border of about a ½-inch around. Then take the unbuttered side and flip it over the middle. Take the opposite end and fold it over as you would a letter.
5. Now, using a bench scraper, turn the dough and sprinkle with flour. Flip and dust again. Then repeat Step 3 and create a square, ⅛-inch in thickness. Take your spatula and spread another ⅓ of the softened butter. Then fold the dough into thirds. Place onto a lined baking tray and place into the freezer for ten minutes or until the butter is chilled.
6. Remove from the fridge and dust with flour. Shape the dough into a square a little thicker than ⅛ of an inch. Spread the remaining ⅓ butter over the square. Leave a 1inch border on the top edge. Place your finger in some water and lightly wet the unbuttered edge. Roll the dough into a log shape beginning from the bottom edge. Sprinkle with more flour and neaten up the ends if necessary. Cover completely with plastic wrap and place in the fridge overnight.
7. To make the sugar syrup, add the sugar, water, lemon zest, and cinnamon in a medium-sized pot. Bring to the boil over low to medium heat. Do not stir. Remove from the stove when the syrup gets between 210 to 215 degrees F (100 degrees C).
8. Now preheat the oven to 550 degrees F (288 degrees C). Lightly grease a muffin tin.

9. In a chilled pot, whisk together the flour, cold milk, and salt. Cook over low to medium heat until the milk begins to thicken. You must whisk continuously. After about 5 minutes remove from the stove and allow it to cool for 15 minutes.
10. Once the mixture has cooled, whisk in the 6 egg yolks. Add the vanilla and sugar syrup and mix. Place custard into a large glass measuring jug.
11. Remove the dough from the fridge and neaten up any ragged or uneven ends. Using a sharp knife divide the log into 12 equal portions.
12. Place each of the 12 pieces of dough into the greased muffin cups. Place your thumb into cold water and then gently press the dough into the bottom and the sides of the muffin cup. Make sure the dough reaches at least ⅛-inch above the top of the muffin cup. Pour custard into each cup filling them ¾ of the way.
13. Bake in the preheated oven until the custard starts to caramelize and darken and the pastry browns (10-12 minutes in total). Cool slightly and serve warm.

## Tips

The vanilla, cinnamon, and lemon zest are all optional. You can add one or all three.

## Tools

Large mixing bowl, silicone spatula, rolling pin, medium-sized pot, plastic wrap, thermometer, 12-cup muffin pan, stovetop, measuring jug, sharp knife

# Greek Baklava

Ready in **1hr 30 minutes**

Serves **18 people**

**393 calories** per serving

### History

Who can truly lay claim to the Baklava is a contested matter. While Greece claims to have invented this delicious, flaky pastry so do a host of other countries. Its origins date back to the eighth century A.D. in Assyria. It was reserved for very special occasions.

### Ingredients

Dough:

- 1 pound (450g) of phyllo dough
- 1 pound (450g) chopped nuts
- 1 cup of softened butter
- 1 teaspoon of ground cinnamon
- 1 cup of water
- 1 cup of white sugar
- 1 teaspoon of vanilla essence
- ½ cup of honey

**Preparation**

1. First, preheat the oven to 350 degrees F (175 degrees C). Grease a 9 x13 inch pan.
2. Chop the nuts and then toss together with the ground cinnamon. Put aside.
3. Unroll phyllo pastry dough. Cut the entire stack in half so that they fit in the pan. Cover the phyllo pastry with a lightly moistened cloth so that it does not dry out. Then put two sheets of dough in the pan and butter them both well. Repeat this step until you have 8 sheets in total, layered on top of one another. Sprinkle with two tablespoons of the nut/cinnamon mixture. Repeat by layering the phyllo pastry, butter, and nuts/cinnamon mixture until you have a stack that is 6 - 8 sheets thick.
4. Use a knife to cut into shapes, either square or diamonds. You must make sure you cut all the way to the base of the pan. Bake for around 45-50 minutes. The baklava will be a nice golden color and crisp.
5. While the Baklava is in the oven, boil sugar and water together in a pot over medium heat. When the sugar has melted add honey and vanilla essence. Simmer for 15-20 minutes.
6. Take the baklava from the oven and spoon sauce over it immediately. Let cool and enjoy.

**Tips**

Once it's baked be sure not to cover up your baklava otherwise it will get soggy.

**Tools**

Oven, 9 x 13-inch pan, mixing bowl, medium-sized pot, sharp knife, measuring cups, moist cloth

# Italian Cannoli

Ready in **3 hrs 45 minutes**

Serves **30 people**

**401 calories** per serving

### History

Cannoli is an Italian dessert that comes from Sicily. It is a sweet pastry that is traditionally filled with either ricotta or mascarpone cheese and flavored with pistachios, rose water, Marsala wine, and candied fruit. It was first baked in the capital of Palermo to celebrate the end of lent known as Carnivale.

**Ingredients**

Shells:

- 3 cups of flour (all-purpose)
- 1 egg
- 1 egg yolk
- ¼ cup of white sugar
- ¼ teaspoon of ground cinnamon
- 3 tablespoons of shortening
- ½ cup of sweet Marsala wine
- 1 tablespoon of white vinegar (distilled)
- 2 tablespoons of water
- 1 egg white
- Oil for frying

Filling:

- 4 cups of ricotta cheese or mascarpone cheese
- ½ cup of confectioners' sugar
- 1 teaspoon of lemon zest
- ½ dark chocolate, chopped

## Preparation

1. In a medium-sized mixing bowl, add the flour, the sugar, and cinnamon together. Then slice up the shortening into pea-size pieces. Make a small well in the center of the dry mixture and add in the egg, the egg yolk, the wine, distilled vinegar, and the water. Mix together using a fork. When you have stiff dough, turn it out onto a clean, floured surface, and knead by hand. Feel free to add more water as needed. Knead the dough by hand for 8-10 minutes. Then cover with a cloth and place in the fridge for 2 hours.
2. After the 2 hours, separate the cannoli dough into three equal size pieces. Then using the palm of your hand, flatten each third enough to be able to pass it through a pasta machine. Roll the dough through the machine until you come to the thinnest setting. Sprinkle lightly with flour if needed. Then put the sheet of cannoli dough on a floured surface. Using a round cookie cutter or even a big large glass, cut out 5-inch circles. Sprinkle the circles with flour. Lastly, roll the dough around cannoli tubes, and secure the edges with a bit of egg whitewash.
3. In a large skillet or even a deep-fryer, heat up the oil to 375 degrees F (190 degrees C). Place the shells into the oil and fry for 2 to 3 minutes, until they are golden-brown in color. Use a pair of tongs. Once cooked, delicately remove and put on a cooling rack over paper towels. Cool just long enough that you can handle the tubes, then carefully twist the tube to remove the shell. Using a tea towel may help you get a better grip. Wash or wipe off the tubes, and use them for more shells.
4. To make the filling, stir together the ricotta cheese and confectioners' sugar using a spoon. Fold in lemon zest and chocolate. Use a pastry bag to pipe into shells, filling from the center to one end, and then doing the same from the other side. Dust with additional confectioners' sugar and grated chocolate for garnish when serving.

## Tips

Don't try to make Cannoli without the proper tubes; they can be bought from most kitchen-themed stores.

## Tools

Oven, 9 x 13-inch pan, mixing bowl, medium-sized pot, sharp knife, measuring cups, Cannoli tubes

# Israeli Sufganiyot

Ready in **3hr 15minutes**

Serves **30 people**

**141 calories** per serving

### History

Sufganiya is the Israeli take on the doughnut, except without the hole. This favorite is often eaten during Hanukkah and is considered to be a traditional Israeli food. In the past it had savory fillings like mushrooms and cheese but now jam or jelly is most often used.

**Ingredients**

Dough:

- 2 cups flour (all purpose)
- Additional flour for dusting and rolling
- ¼ cup white sugar
- 2 ¼ teaspoons of dry active yeast
- ½ teaspoon salt
- 2 egg yolks
- ¾ cup warm milk
- 2 tablespoons unsalted butter (room temperature)
- 6 cups vegetable oil
- ⅔ cup smooth jelly or jam
- A bit of icing sugar to dust

**Preparation**

1. Put the dry ingredients (flour, sugar, salt, and yeast) into a large mixing bowl. Whisk together. Then add the egg yolks and the warm milk. Fit the hook attachment to your electric mixer and mix together on low-medium speed for one minute or until the dough begins to form and pull together. Then add all the butter on medium-high speed for five minutes until the dough is elastic and smooth in appearance.
2. Grease a big bowl with oil. Take the dough out of the mixing bowl and shape into a ball. Then place the dough ball into the greased bowl and turn it over so that the whole surface is coated in oil. Cover the bowl with a slightly moistened towel. Allow it to rise in a warm place for an hour to an hour and a half. The dough will have doubled in size.
3. Prepare a baking tray by lightly dusting it with flour. Once the dough has risen sufficiently degas it and place on a floured counter. Roll the dough out until it is a ¼-inch in thickness. Take a cookie cutter or even a glass and cut out circles of dough, as many as you can. Transfer the rounds to the floured baking tray, leaving a gap between them of about ½-inch. Repeat until you have 30 rounds. Cover with your moist towel and allow it to rest for an additional half an hour until the rounds have puffed up.
4. Using a thick-bottomed pot heat up your oil to 350 degrees F. Place your jelly/jam into your piping bag. Being careful not to deflate the rounds, take a spatula and delicately place them in the oil. Make sure to leave some space between them and cook about 5-6 at a time. Fry the dough until the bottom half is a nice golden brown color, then flip them over and fry the other side (it's about 1 ½ minute on either side). Remove and place on a baking rack.
5. Once you have finished frying your donuts wait for them to cool down before adding the jelly/jam. Pierce each donut with a sharp knife and then squeeze a teaspoon of jelly/jam. Lightly dust with the powdered sugar

**Tips**

If you don't have a cookie-cutter you can use the rim of a glass.

**Tools**

Electric mixer, cookie-cutter, thermometer, pastry bag, moist towel, spatula, slotted spoon, knife, bowls, pot, baking tray

# Austrian Linzer Torte

Ready in **65 minutes**

Serves **8 people**

**343 calories** per serving

### History

Linzer Torte is thought to be one of the oldest cakes in the whole of human history. The first record of the torte dates all the way back to the 1600s. It was mass-produced by a man named Johann Konrad Vogel in 1823. He lived in the village of Linz, hence the name. The torte is famous for its latticework and deliciously nutty, fruity flavor.

### Ingredients

- 2 cups of flour (all-purpose)
- 2 cups of hazelnuts (ground)
- ½ cup of white sugar
- ½ cup of brown sugar
- 1 teaspoon of cinnamon (ground)
- Pinch of salt
- Pinch of cloves
- 1 cup butter, (cold and cubed)
- 2 eggs (beaten)
- 1 teaspoon of grated lemon zest
- 1⅓ cups of raspberry jam (seedless)
- Icing sugar for dusting

### Preparation

1. In a big bowl, add all of the dry ingredients. Then add the cubed butter and mix until the dough has a crumb-like texture. Then add the two beaten eggs and the lemon zest. Mix together. Then separate the dough into four pieces. Cover them and place in the fridge until chilled (3 hours).
2. Once the dough is chilled, take two pieces of dough from the fridge; press them each into a 9-inch fluted tart pan (untreated). The pan should have a removable bottom. Then spread about ⅔ or a cup of jam over each piece.
3. Prepare two sheets of wax paper by lightly dusting them with flour. Then roll one piece of the remaining dough between the sheets. Roll into a rectangle shape about 10 x 6 inches. Then cut the rectangle into 6 strips about 1 inch in width. Carefully arrange the strips in a lattice design over the spread jam. Repeat this with the last portion of dough.
4. Bake the tortes at 350 degrees F (175 degrees C) for 45 minutes or until the crust has gone brown and the jam has bubbled. Cool and dust with icing sugar.

### Tips

Linzer torte is usually made with red raspberry jam but you can use apricot or plum jam instead.

### Tools

Mixing bowls, 2 x fluted tart pans, wax paper, rolling pin, butter knife, sharp knife

# South African Koeksisters

Ready in **50 minutes**

Serves **4-6 people**

**552 calories** per serving

### History

Koeksisters originated from the Afrikaans communities of South Africa. They are beloved by the South African people but are dangerously sweet so it is ill-advised to eat more than one Koeksister at a sitting.

### Ingredients

Syrup:

- 1 cup of water
- 2 ½ cups white sugar
- 2 ½ teaspoons of lemon juice
- 1 teaspoon of vanilla essence

Dough:

- 1 ½ cups flour (cake)
- 4 ½ teaspoons of baking powder
- ¼ teaspoon of salt
- 4 tablespoons of butter
- ⅔ cup of milk
- 3 cups of canola oil

**Preparation**

1. Place the water and sugar in a medium-sized pot and allow it to simmer on a low heat. Stir continuously until all of the sugar has dissolved (+/- 7 minutes). Take the pot off of the stove and add the vanilla essence and the lemon juice. Place the pot into the refrigerator to cool.
2. In a large mixing bowl combine the flour, salt and the baking powder. Whisk together. Add the butter and mix. Then add the milk and mix again until it forms nice dough.
3. Roll out the dough until you have a thickness of a ¼- inch (5mm). Then slice the dough into ½-inch strips (10mm). Take 3 of the strips and join them together at one end. Plait the strips together and join again at the other end.
4. Heat up the oil in a large pot. Cook 3 - 4 Koeksisters at once. Fry both sides until they are a rich golden color. Remove from the oil and dip them into the cool syrup. Place on a wire baking rack to allow the extra syrup to run off. Refrigerator and eat once cool.

**Tips**

The syrup must stay cold so make sure you leave it in the fridge in-between dipping.

**Tools**

Mixing bowls, pot, whisk, wire baking rack

# Cuban Pastelitos

Ready in **1hr 20 minutes**

Serves **16 people**

**170 calories** per serving

### History

Pastelitos is a popular Cuban puff pastry made with either savory or sweet fillings. These can include guava, pineapple, cream cheese and coconut, as well as savory fillings such as ham, beef, and chicken.

### Ingredients

- 16-ounces (450g) Guava shells (canned in syrup)
- ½ cup water, plus additional water as needed
- 1 ½ cups of butter
- ½ teaspoon of salt
- 3 ⅓ cups of flour (all-purpose)
- 1 egg, (beaten with 1 tablespoon of water)
- 1 ½ tablespoons of syrup

**Preparation**

1. Blend the guava together in a blender until smooth. Then cook on a low-medium heat until thick. Allow to cool. Spoon the guava into a pastry bag.
2. In a mixing bowl, add ½ cup of water, 3 tablespoons of butter and a ½ teaspoon of salt. Mix together until smooth. Add the flour and combine. Add water as needed to form a medium to hard dough. Shape into a ball and allow it to rest for 20 minutes.
3. After the dough has rested roll it out to form a square, ½-inch thick. Take the remaining butter and place it in the middle of the square. Fold the four corners inward like an envelope to cover the butter. Sprinkle with flour and roll to form a rectangle shape, ¼-inch thick. Then fold a third of the dough into the middle and the remaining third over those two. Allow the dough to sit for 15 minutes. Then repeat the process again twice, allowing the dough to rest for 15 minutes in between each roll.
4. Preheat your oven to 350 degrees F (175 degrees C).
5. Now roll out a rectangle, ⅛-inch thick. Use a knife to cut up the rectangle into a 4-inch wide strip the same length as your baking sheet.
6. Place the strip on a wax-lined baking tray. Take your guava filling and spread it across the strip. Then cut another strip of the same length and press the edges together. Egg-wash the tops and place in the preheated oven for 35 minutes. Remove them from the oven and brush each one with syrup. Then bake for an additional 5 minutes. Once baked, slice crosswise into 16 sections.

**Tips**

The syrup must stay cold so make sure you leave it in the fridge in-between dipping.

**Tools**

Mixing bowls, pot, whisk, wire baking rack

# Dutch Bossche Bollens

Ready in **2hr 20 minutes**

Serves **6 people**

**400 calories** per serving

History

Bossche Bollens come from the Den Boll, which is a Dutch town. This delicious pastry was first made in the 1920s by two rival bakers. The bakers' rivalry resulted in the perfection which is the Bossche Bol.

**Ingredients**

- ⅖ cup of water
- 3 tablespoons of butter
- ½ teaspoon of salt
- ⅖ cup flour (all-purpose)
- 4 eggs (need 2 whole eggs & 2 egg whites)
- 1 cup of whipping cream
- 2 tablespoons icing sugar
- 1 vanilla pod
- ⅞ cup icing sugar
- 2 tablespoons of cocoa powder (unsweetened)

**Preparation**

1. In a cast iron saucepan or heavy-bottomed pot bring the butter, water, and salt to a boil. In a mixing bowl, add the flour. Then add the flour to the boiling water, remembering to stir continuously. Stir until a ball of dough forms.
2. Remove the pot or pan from the stove and add two eggs one at a time. Only add the second egg once the first one has been properly mixed into the dough. Stop stirring when the dough is shiny.
3. Now separate the dough ball into six smaller balls. Place these on a greased baking tray. Preheat the oven to 437 degrees F (225 degrees C). Bake the rolls for 20 minutes. Once they are a nice golden brown color, switch the oven off and open the door a little. Leave the rolls inside for 10 minutes to cool.
4. While you are waiting you can combine the 2 tablespoons icing sugar with 1 egg white and ½ of the seeds from the vanilla pod with the cream. Beat until stiff.
5. In another bowl add the icing sugar and cocoa. Then add the second egg white. Fill your piping bag with the cream. Then make a small hole in the pastry, place the nozzle of the bag in and fill each one with cream. Lastly, brush the tops of the pastry with the cocoa-icing sugar-egg white mixture.

**Tips**

For a truly authentic recipe only use unsweetened Dutch cocoa

**Tools**

Mixing bowls, pot, whisk, piping bag, baking tray, cast iron saucepan

# Spanish Churros

Ready in **30 minutes**

Serves **6 people**

**756 calories** per serving

### History

The history of Churros dates back all the way to the 1500s when the Spanish arrived in South America during the Spanish Inquisition. Around that time cocoa was also making its mark on the world and so the Spanish formulated a chocolate sauce perfect for dunking Churros.

**Ingredients**

- 1 cup of water
- 1 tablespoon of vegetable oil
- Pinch of salt
- 1 teaspoon of sugar
- 1 cup of flour ( white)
- ¼ teaspoon baking powder
- Sugar/ honey (optional)
- Oil

**Preparation**

1. Pour about 2-inches of oil into a pan. Turn on the heat up to a medium-high. You want to fry the Churros between 350 to 375 degrees F (170 – 195 degrees C)
2. Then, in another saucepan, add the water, a tablespoon of vegetable oil, sugar, and salt. Put the lid on and bring to boil.
3. In a mixing bowl, combine the flour and the baking powder.
4. When the water mixture has come to a boil, pour it slowly into the flour mixture. Remember to stir continuously. You want to achieve smooth dough with no lumps.
5. Then spoon the smooth dough into a churrera or a pastry bag.
6. When your oil has reached the desired temperature gently squeeze the dough into the hot oil. Fry the dough until it is a golden brown.
7. Then take the Churro out with a slotted spoon. Allow the excess oil to drain on a paper towel or wire baking rack. Cut them into desired lengths using a sharp knife.
8. Then you may drizzle some honey over the Churros or dust with sugar.

**Tips**

A churrera is also known as a large cookie press.

**Tools**

Mixing bowls, pot, whisk, wire baking rack, paper towel, slotted spoon, sharp knife, cookie press or pastry bag, 2 x saucepans

# American Donuts

Ready in **90 minutes**

Serves **10 people**

**303 calories** per serving

### History

Donuts are undoubtedly a huge part of American culture. Their history can be traced all the way back to the early days of New York, or New Amsterdam as it was known then. The Dutch settlers arrived with their olykoeks . It was, however, an American by the name of Hanson Gregory who claimed to have invented the donut with the hole in 1847 when he was 16 years old.

**Ingredients**

For the Dough:

- 4 cups of flour (all-purpose)
-  cup of sugar +1
- 1 teaspoon of salt
- 1 ½ tablespoon of yeast
- ¼ cup butter (room temperature)
- 2 medium-sized eggs
- 1 ¼ cups milk (warm)
- Oil for frying

Dusting:

- Sugar or icing sugar

**Preparation**

1. Add the flour, sugar, salt, and yeast in a large mixing bowl and combine. Then add the warm milk and eggs. Knead with a dough hook until you have achieved smooth dough. It needs to be sticky but workable. Add more flour or milk to get the dough to the right consistency.
2. Place the dough into a greased bowl and make sure to turn it over so that the whole surface is greased. Cover with a cloth and leave to rise until it is doubled in size (+/- 1hour).
3. After about an hour degas the dough by punching it. Cover the dough for a second time and leave for 50-60minutes to rise again.
4. After the second rise, place the dough on a floured work surface. Roll it into a rectangle of about ½ inch thick. If you have a doughnut cutter use it to cut the dough otherwise use a glass and the cap of a small bottle to cut out the correct shape. Delicately move the donuts to a tray lined with a towel. Cover and leave for half an hour.
5. If there are scraps, press them into a ball and leave them for 20 minutes before rolling and cutting them out.
6. Use a frying pan to heat 2 inches of oil. Make sure to heat it on a medium setting. Carefully slide the donuts off of the tray and into the oil. They will only take about 2 or 3 minutes to cook. Make sure to only turn them once. Once cooked, place them on a wire rack or in a strainer to drain away any of the excess oil.
7. Warm doughnuts should be dipped in granulated sugar or dusted with confectioners' sugar. They can be served both warm or at room temperature.

**Tips**

Test the heat of the oil by placing a scrap of dough into the pot; the oil should start to bubble.

**Tools**

Electric mixer, dough hook, mixing bowls, wire baking rack, baking tray, cloth

# Finnish Joulutorttu

Ready in **1hr 12 minutes**

Serves **12 people**

**183 calories** per serving

### History

Finish Joulutorttu are baked every year at Christmas time. They are a rich combination of flaky pastry, ricotta cheese, plum jam, and icing sugar. The Finnish are fond of having these delicious treats with a cup of mulled wine.

**Ingredients**

For the Pastry

- 16 tablespoons of butter, (salted and softened)
- 1 cup of ricotta cheese
- 2 cups of flour (all-purpose)
- For the cookies
- ½ cup of prune jam (or another thick jam of your choosing)
- 1 large egg (beaten)
- Icing sugar (for dusting)

### Preparation

1. In a large mixing bowl combine the butter with the ricotta cheese using a stand mixer or even an electric hand mixer. Then add in the flour, and combine until it comes together to form a soft dough.
2. Now separate the dough into two pieces. Shape each piece into a ball and cover each ball in a layer of plastic wrap. Place in the fridge for 2-3 hours (or overnight), until the dough is firm.
3. Preheat your oven to 425 degrees F (220 degrees C). Lightly dust your work surface with flour and then roll out one ball of dough into a rectangle shape about 12 x 9 inches roughly ⅛ inch thick. Then slice the rectangle into 3-inch squares. In each of the squares, make four cuts into the dough. The cut should go from each corner and ½ way to the middle of the square. Then put 1 teaspoon of your jam into the middle of each square. Fold the corners of the square over the jam. Then lightly wash with beaten egg and gently press the corners together over the jam. Make sure you seal it adequately so the jam doesn't leak out.
4. Prepare a baking sheet by lining it with baking paper. Place the cookies about an inch apart. Repeat the process with the second ball of the dough.
5. Lightly wash the tops of all the cookies with the beaten egg.
6. Place the cookies in the oven and bake for 10-12 minutes, until they are golden.
7. Remove from the oven and allow them to cool for 5 minutes, before moving them to a wire rack.
8. Only when the cookies are cool, lightly dust with icing sugar.

### Tips

Try to prepare the dough the day before so that it can rest the whole night in the fridge.

### Tools

Mixing bowls, wire baking rack, pastry brush, sharp knife, teaspoon, plastic wrap

# Austrian Apple Strudel

Ready in **65 minutes**

Serves **6 people**

**229 calories** per serving

### History

Apple Strudel is one of Austria's pride
and joys and it's easy to see why. This
delicious pastry was first believed to
have been made in Hungary and then
brought to Austria by the Ottomans who
often visited.

**Ingredients**

- ⅓cup of raisins
- 2 tablespoons of water
- ¼ teaspoon of almond extract
- 3 cups of chopped and peeled apples
- ⅓ cup + 2 teaspoons sugar (divided)
- 3 tablespoons flour (all-purpose)
- ¼ teaspoon cinnamon (ground)
- 2 tablespoons of salted butter (softened)
- 2 tablespoons of canola oil

- 8 sheets of phyllo dough (size: 14 x 9-inch)
- Icing sugar (to dust)

## Preparation

1. Preheat your oven to 350 degrees F (175 degrees C). Put your raisins, water, and almond extract into a large microwave-friendly bowl. Place into the microwave and cook, uncovered, for 1 ½ minutes on high. Allow to stand and cool for 5 minutes. Add your apples, ⅓ cup of sugar, flour, and the ground cinnamon and combine.
2. In a medium-sized bowl, combine your melted butter and oil. Take out 2 teaspoons of the mixture for later. Take one sheet of phyllo dough and place it on your work surface. Then brush with the butter/oil mixture. Make sure the rest of the pastry is covered with a moist cloth to stop it from drying out. Repeat the process until you have layered all of the 8 phyllo sheets. Spoon the apple mixture onto the phyllo and then spread it within two inches of one side.
3. Gently take the short edges and fold them over the filling. Roll it up like a Swiss roll, starting from the side with a 2-inch border. Place onto a prepared baking sheet. Brush with the butter-oil mixture and sprinkle with sugar. Using a sharp knife, score the top by cutting diagonal slits into the top of strudel.
4. Bake the strudel until golden, about 35 to 40 minutes. Allow it to cool on a wire rack. Dust with icing sugar.

## Tips

Apple Strudel is best served warm with some whipped cream or ice-cream.

## Tools

Baking tray, microwaveable bowl, mixing bowl, sharp knife, wire baking rack, pastry brush, moist cloth

# French Croissant

Ready in **5 hours**

Serves **15 people**

**294 calories** per serving

### History

There is nothing quite as French as a croissant which is why it is interesting to learn that the croissant actually originated in Austria. It was first baked in 1683 to celebrate the victory of the Christians over the Ottomans.

**Ingredients**

- 4 cups flour (all-purpose)
- ⅓ cup of sugar
- 2 1/5 teaspoons of salt
- 5 teaspoons of dry, active yeast
- 1 ¼ cups of butter (cubed and cold)
- 1 cup of milk
- 1 large egg (make an egg wash by beating with a teaspoon of water)

**Preparation**

1. In a large bowl, add the flour, sugar, yeast, and salt and mix together until they are combined.
2. Add your cubed butter to the flour. Then add your milk and combine them all together to form firm dough.
3. Roll it into a ball and cover it with plastic wrap. Place in the fridge and allow the dough to chill for about an hour.
4. After an hour, roll the dough out onto a floured workspace. You can use a rolling pin to create a long rectangle. Then fold your dough into thirds. Think of it like folding a letter. Then turn your dough 90 degrees and repeat the fold 4 more times. You'll notice the dough probably has streaks of butter in it.
5. Rewrap the dough and place back in the fridge for another hour. After an hour unwrap the dough and separate it into two equal sized pieces. Use your rolling pin to create two rectangles roughly ⅛-inch thick. The size of the rectangle should be 10-inches (wide) x 22-inches (long). Then cut the rectangles into triangles, roughly 5-inches at the widest end.
6. Notch the widest side of each of the triangles with a cut about ½-inch. From the wide end roll the dough all the way to the pointed end. Then tuck the pointed end under your croissant.
7. Prepare a baking tray by lining it with backing paper. Place your croissants on the tray and cover with plastic wrap. Leave to rest for 1 to 2 hours.
8. Preheat your oven to 375 degrees F (190 degrees C). Use a basting brush to lightly egg wash your croissants.
9. Place in the oven and bake until they are puffed up, flaky and a nice golden brown color (15 - 20 minutes).

**Tips**

In order to have successful croissants the dough must remain chilled while folding. If it starts to soften up, place it back in the fridge for a while.

**Tools**

Basting brush, rolling pin, mixing bowls, baking tray, cling wrap, baking paper, ruler, sharp knife

**RECIPE**

# Taiwanese Pineapple Cake

Ready in **1hr 40 minutes**

Serves **24 people**

**111 calories** per serving

### History

Feng Li Su also called Taiwanese pineapple cakes are a very famous pastry which originated in Taiwan. These treats are comparable to shortbread with a delicious pineapple filling. Feng Li Su is often eaten during Lunar New Year.

**Ingredients**

- 1 cup of butter (unsalted and at room temperature
- ¼ cup of icing sugar
- 2 eggs
- ½ teaspoon vanilla essence
- 2½ cups flour (all-purpose)
- ¼ cup of cornstarch
- Pinch of salt
- 1 cup of pineapple jam

## Preparation

1. In a mixing bowl, add your butter and icing sugar. On a medium-speed and using the mixers paddle attachment, cream the butter and icing sugar together until fluffy.
2. Then add the eggs and combine. Next add the vanilla essence and combine.
3. In another bowl, add the flour and the salt. Add to the mixing bowl and combine. Your dough should be quite soft and workable.
4. Wrap the dough in plastic wrap and place in the fridge for half an hour.
5. Preheat your oven to 325 degrees F (160 degrees C). Prepare several baking trays with baking paper.
6. Once the dough is firm, roll it into 1-inch balls and then place on baking trays. With the palm of your hand, flatten the balls out and spoon 1 teaspoon of the pineapple jam in the middle.
7. Gently pinch the ends of the dough around the jam in order to seal it.
8. Bake for 20 minutes, until cakes are a lovely golden brown color. Lastly, place them on a wire baking rack.

## Tips

You can make your own pineapple jam by boiling down chopped-up pineapple in a pot with water and then adding sugar.

## Tools

Electric mixer, paddle attachment for mixer, mixing bowls, baking trays, baking paper, teaspoon

# Japanese Mochi

Ready in **3hrs 35minutes**

Serves **8 people**

**213 calories** per serving

### History

The processes of making Mochi first originated in China, however it was during the Heian Period in Japan (794–1192), where Mochi was considered a "food for the gods' '. It was also used as an offering in religious rituals.

### Ingredients

- 1 cup of red bean paste (sweetened)
- 1 cup of sweet rice flour (also called mochiko)
- 1 teaspoon of green tea powder (also called matcha)
- 1 cup of water (room temperature)
- ¼ cup of white sugar
- ½ cup of cornstarch

**Preparation**

1. First, you need to wrap your bean paste in some aluminum foil. Then put it in the freezer for a minimum of three hours.
2. In a microwave- friendly bowl, combine the rice flour and the matcha together. Add the water and then the sugar. Combine until the mixture is smooth. Then cover the bowl with some plastic wrap.
3. Place the mixture into the microwave and cook on high for three and a half minutes. While you wait take the bean paste from the freezer and separate it into 8 equal-sized balls.
4. After the three and a half minutes take the mixture out of the microwave and stir. Heat the mixture again for thirty seconds.
5. Lightly flour your counter with your cornstarch. The Mochi should be hot when you roll it into balls. You can measure the size of the balls between two tablespoons. Once you've rolled the balls, flatten them with the palm of your hand and place a ball of bean paste in the middle. You want the Mochi to cover the bean paste entirely, and by using your fingers, gently pinch the Mochi around the bean paste. Use your cornstarch to make sure they don't stick. Repeat until all the bean paste and Mochi is finished.
6. Place your finished Mochi seam-down on a piece of baking paper.

**Tips**

The dough is very sticky so be sure to dust the counter and your hands well.

**Tools**

Baking paper, microwaveable bowl, aluminum foil, cling wrap, tablespoons

# Filipino Pastillas de Leche

Ready in **11 minutes**

Serves **4 people**

**76 calories** per serving

## History

Hailing from the town of San Miguel in the Philippines this special dish even has its own festival.

## Ingredients

- 2 cups of powdered milk
- 1 can of condensed milk
- ½ cup of sugar

**Preparation**

1. In a large mixing bowl, add your condensed milk
2. Then fold in your powdered milk gradually to create dough.
3. Mold the mixture into cylinder-like shapes. Then sprinkle each one with sugar.
4. Wrap the cylinders in baking paper and refrigerate.

**Tips**

Allow to set properly before serving

**Tools**

Large mixing bowl, paddle, baking paper

# Brazilian Bolo de Rolo

Ready in **65 minutes**

Serves **6 people**

**229 calories** per serving

## History

Bolo de Rolo is a cake all the way from the Pernambuco state in Brazil. It most resembles the famous Swiss roll, and is usually eaten at breakfast or for dessert.

**Ingredients**

- 1 cup of sugar
- 1 cup of flour (all-purpose and sifted)
- 1 cup of butter (softened)
- 5 eggs (at room temp)
- 1 teaspoon of vanilla essence
- ¼ teaspoon of salt
- ½ cup of Guava paste (for filling)

**Preparation**

1. In a bowl beat the egg whites into stiff peaks. In another bowl, combine the cup of sugar and the softened butter. Then add the egg yolks one at a time. Add the vanilla essence and the egg whites. Fold in.
2. Prepare your shallow pans by lining it with baking paper. Separate the mixture into five and then spread the mixture thinly. Preheat your oven to 350 degrees F (180 degrees C). Bake each cake separately. The cake should be golden in color.
3. Once each cake is baked neaten the edges and spread your filling across it. Then wrap it up quickly using a kitchen towel. Repeat with the next four layers. After about 20 minutes you can unroll the kitchen towel. Cut into slices and enjoy.

**Tips**

If you don't want to use guava paste you can replace it with Nutella.

**Tools**

5 x shallow pans, electric mixer, two bowls, baking paper, kitchen towel

# Indian Jalebi

Ready in **50 minutes**

Serves **10 people**

**454 calories** per serving

**History**

These syrupy spirals originated in India in the 15th century. They are still incredibly popular today.

**Ingredients**

- 3 cups of flour (all-purpose)
- ½ cup of corn flour
- 2 cups of hung curd
- 1 ½ teaspoons of baking powder
- ½ cup of Ghee (or butter)
- 2 cups of vegetable oil
- 3 cups of sugar
- 3 cups of water
- 5 strands of saffron
- 4 drops of rose essence
- ½ teaspoon of green cardamom (powdered)
- ½ teaspoon of food color

## Preparation

1. Combine the flour, corn flour and baking powder in a large mixing bowl. Then add the ghee as well as the food color to the mix. Lastly add the water and the hung curd. The batter should be thick. Cover and leave to ferment overnight.
2. For the syrup, place a pan over a low-medium heat. Place the water into the pan and heat. Then add the sugar and allow it to dissolve entirely. Simmer the mixture until the consistency is stringy. Then add the rose essence, cardamom and saffron. Stir.
3. Heat your vegetable oil in a pot. You can use a pastry bag or even just a piece of muslin cloth, fill it with the batter and then cut a small hole in the top of the muslin cloth. Squeeze the batter out in a spiral shape to make concentric circles. Work from the inside out. Fry the batter until it is golden
4. Now, heat oil in a pan over medium flame for deep frying. Fill the Jalebi batter in a muslin cloth and pierce a small hole in the cloth. Squeeze the muslin cloth to make concentric circles. Move from inside to outside to make perfect circles. Fry till Jalebis are crisp and golden.
5. Next take the crispy Jalebi and dip them in the syrup for 3 minutes. Make sure the setup has cooled sufficiently. Place them on a tray lined with paper.

## Tips

Make sure the batter isn't too runny or too thick. It needs to be squeezed easily through the cloth. Also mind the oil is not too hot otherwise the Jalebis will cook too quickly on the outside and will be undercooked on the inside.

## Tools

Muslin cloth (or piping bag), pot, saucepan, bowls, paper towel

# Turkish Künefe

Ready in **55minutes**

Serves **4 people**

**508 calories** per serving

## History

Nothing beats this Turkish pastry which is a delightful combination of sweet and savory. While its origins are debated it is believed to date all the way back to the 10th century.

## Ingredients

Syrup:

- cup of water
- 1 cup of sugar
- 1 slice of lemon

Künefe:

- 2 cups of raw, shredded kadayif dough
- ½ cup of butter (+ extra to grease pans)
- 1 cup of mozzarella cheese
- 1 tablespoon of pistachios (ground)

**Preparation**

1. Begin by making the syrup. In a medium-sized pot add the sugar, water and the slice of lemon. Bring the mixture to a boil. Once bubbles start to appear, reduce the heat and allow the mixture to simmer for 15-20 minutes. You'll know it's ready once it's thickened. Allow the syrup to cool down.
2. In another pot, melt the butter and allow it to cool. Cover the kadayif noodles with the butter.
3. Prepare your pans by greasing them in butter (pans should be 9-inch).
4. Spread the noodles in the greased pans, making sure you spread them evenly.
5. Cover the noodles in the shredded cheese.
6. On a low heat, cook the cheesy noodles until they are a nice, golden-brown color. Then flip and cook on the other side.
7. Repeat until you've cooked both portions.
8. Once cooked, spoon the cool syrup over them. Sprinkle the ground pistachios on top.

**Tips**

Always serve immediately.

**Tools**

2 x 9-inch pans, pots, knife, wooden spoon

# Swedish Kanelbulle

Ready in **2hrs 37minutes**

Serves **40 people**

**103 calories** per serving

### History

Kanelbulle is a very famous Swedish pastry which we know in English as a cinnamon roll. October 4th in Sweden is Cinnamon Roll Day.

**Ingredients**

Dough:

- 2 ½ cups of full cream milk
- 1 ½ cups of butter (melted)
- 1 cup of sugar
- 1 teaspoon of salt
- 2 teaspoons freshly ground cardamom
- 4 ½ teaspoons active dry yeast
- 8 to 9 cups flour (all-purpose)

Filling:

- ⅓ cup of butter (melted)
- ⅔ cup of sugar
- 2 tablespoons of ground cinnamon
- 1 egg beaten with 2 tablespoons of water ( egg wash)
- Toasted sliced almonds

**Preparation**

1. In a saucepan, heat up the milk until it starts to gently boil, as soon as bubbles appear turn it off. Then add the sugar, salt, melted butter and ground cardamom to the milk. Allow it to cool enough so you can touch it but it's still warm.
2. Stir in the dry yeast and allow the mixture to rest for 10 minutes.
3. After 10 minutes it's time to add the flour. Use an electric mixer and the paddle hook attachment. Add the flour ½ cup at a time. After 5 cups exchange the paddle for the dough hook attachment and use it for the remaining cups of flour.
4. Cover and allow dough to rise for an hour until the dough has doubled in size.
5. Degas the dough by punching it down. Place on a lightly floured workspace and knead gently until shiny and smooth. Separate into two parts.
6. Roll each part of dough into a rectangle roughly 12 x 18-inches. Take the ⅓ cup of melted butter and generously wash both rectangles.
7. Now make the filling. Take a small- sized bowl and begin by combining the sugar with the ground cinnamon. Then sprinkle it across both rectangles - try to keep the spread even. Then roll it up into a log shape.
8. Use a sharp knife and cut each log into 20 same-sized slices. Put each of the little rolls into a paper cupcake holder and place them all on a baking tray. Now cover with a cloth and allow them to rest for 45 minutes.
9. While the rolls are resting, preheat your oven to 425 degrees F (220 degrees C)
10. After 45minutes, brush your cinnamon rolls with an egg wash and then sprinkle with almonds. Put them in the center of the oven and bake for 6/7 minutes, the rolls should be a golden color and firm.

**Tips**

Make sure to get your filling distribution as evenly as you can.

**Tools**

Rolling pin, mixing bowl, baking tray, sharp knife, measuring cups, cloth, ruler, baking tray, cupcake papers, basting brush

# Danish Kringle

Ready in **24hrs 50minutes**

Serves **12 people**

**410 calories** per serving

### History

Traditionally, Danish Kringles take a number of days to assemble and consist of around 30 layers of delicate pastry. Luckily, this recipe is a simplified version of this delicious Danish dish. Danish Kringles arrived in America in the 1800s and was brought in by immigrant bakers from Denmark.

### Ingredients

- 2 cups of salted butter
- 2 cups of flour (all-purpose)
- 1 cup sour cream (cultured)
- 2 cups of brown sugar
- 1 cup of icing sugar
- 1 ½ cups of walnuts (chopped)
- 1 tablespoon of water

**Preparation**

1. Cube 8 ounces butter and mix in the flour with your finger until it forms a crumb. Mix in the sour cream. Shape the dough into a ball and place in the fridge overnight.
2. Preheat the oven to 375 degrees F (190 degrees C) and prepare a baking tray by greasing lightly.
3. Make the filling by adding 8 ounces butter, 2 ½ cups brown sugar and 8 ounces chopped walnut.
4. Divide the dough into three pieces of equal size. Place two of the pieces into the fridge to keep cool. On a floured counter, roll one part into a rectangle (12 x 17inch). Work on the long edges of the rectangle. Use a sharp knife or blade to cut 4-inch long lines (at an angle) about ½-inch apart. Take ⅓ of the filling and spoon in across the rectangle's uncut middle. Crisscross the filling like a braid. Press the ends of strips together to seal. Top with a sprinkling of the ⅓ walnuts. Repeat with the other two pieces. Then place the Danishes on the baking tray.
5. Bake them for about half an hour until they are a nice golden-brown color. While the Danishes cool, make icing by using the powdered sugar with water. Drizzle over the warm loaves.

**Tips**

You can replace the walnuts with pecans.

**Tools**

Baking tray, sharp knife, ruler, bowls, scale, measuring cups.

**RECIPE**

# Argentinian Alfajores

Ready in **35 minutes**

Serves **24 people**

**153 calories** per serving

## History

Alfajores is a very famous and traditional Argentinian sweet treat which dates back to the 16th century, originally from southern Spain. As immigrants came to the New World these treats made its way to Argentina, and also ended up in Peru to feed hungry Spanish soldiers.

**Ingredients**

Dough:

- 1 cup of flour (all-purpose)
- 1 cup of cornstarch
- 1 teaspoon of baking powder
- ¼ teaspoon of baking soda
- ¼ teaspoon of salt
- ½ cup of sugar
- 8 tablespoons of butter (unsalted and at room temperature)
- 2 egg yolks
- 2 teaspoons of lemon zest (finely grated)

- 1 teaspoon of vanilla essence
- 2 tablespoons of warm water
- 1 cup of coconut (flakes)
- 1 can of condensed milk.

**Preparation**

1. Combine the flour, baking powder, cornstarch, baking soda and salt into a large bowl.
2. Then in your electric mixer combine sugar and the butter. Cream until it is fluffy and light.
3. Add your two egg yolks and mix. Then add your water, vanilla and lemon zest. Mix again.
4. Now add the flour mixture. Beat on quite a low speed until you can see the dough coming together.
5. Roll the dough into a ball and cover completely with plastic wrap. Place in the fridge to rest of a minimum of two hours.
6. Preheat your oven to 350 degrees F (180 degrees C)
7. Prepare a baking tray by lining them with baking paper.
8. After two hours, place the dough onto a floured work surface. Roll it out with a rolling pin until the dough is about ¼-inch in thickness. Use a 2-inch cookie cutter to cut out the dough.
9. Put the cut-outs onto your baking tray and bake. You want the cookies to be a pale yellow on the edges and be firm. (± 10 minutes).
10. Place on a wire baking rack and cool.
11. Spread about one tablespoon of condensed milk onto the cookie and sandwich with another.
12. Roll the sides of the cookie in the coconut before serving. Then dust with icing sugar.

**Tips**

Be sure not to over-bake the cookies. Keep a close eye on them.

**Tools**

Rolling pin, mixing bowl, baking tray, knife, measuring cups, electric mixer, baking trays, baking paper, 2-inch cookie cutter, wire baking rack, ruler

# Czech Koláče

Ready in **55 minutes**

Serves **24 people**

**153 calories** per serving

### History

Koláče originated from the Czech Republic but have become widely popular in America and England due to the immigrant populations. They are traditionally topped with plum jam and poppy seeds. However, modern times have seen a whole variety of new toppings including blueberries, lemons and pineapple.

### Ingredients

- ½ cups of flour (all-purpose)
- ½ cup of semi-coarse flour
- ⅔ cup of milk (lukewarm)
- 1 ½ tablespoons of fresh yeast
- ¼ cup of semolina sugar
- 1 teaspoon of vanilla sugar
- ¼ cup of butter (melted)
- pinch of salt
- 3 eggs
- raisins and almonds
- Plum jam

**Preparation**

1. In a large bowl, mix the semi-coarse and plain flour, make a well in the center and pour ⅔ of the milk into it and the yeast. Combine.
2. Sprinkle the surface with a fine layer of plain flour and a little sugar and leave it in a warm place for 30 minutes to rest. Add both of sugars, salt and eggs, as well as the remaining milk and butter and knead the dough. Mix for 10 minutes at low speed.
3. Remove the dough from the bowl and let it rest for 30 minutes. Divide into pieces (45 g each) and shape into balls in the palm of your hand. Spread them on a baking sheet lined with baking paper. Cover them with a cloth and allow them to rest for another 45 minutes.
4. Use a cookie cutter or the rim of a glass. Brush the cakes with beaten egg. Spread with jam and garnish with raisins and almonds. Allow to rise for 10 minutes.
5. Bake at 320 degrees F (160 degrees C) for 15 minutes.

**Tips**

You can also use cream as a filling or even poppy seeds.

**Tools**

Rolling pin, mixing bowl, baking tray, knife, measuring cups, electric mixer, baking trays, baking paper, , wire baking rack, ruler

# Egyptian Cream Kunāfah

Ready in **60 minutes**

Serves **12 people**

**255 calories** per serving

### History

Egyptian Kunāfah dates all the way back to ancient Egypt. Today it is listed as one of Egypt's national dishes.

### Ingredients

Syrup:

- 2 ¼ cups of sugar
- 1 ¼ cups of water
- 2 tablespoons of orange-blossom water

Filing:

- ⅔ cup of rice flour
- 5 cups of milk
- 4 tablespoons of sugar
- ⅔ cup of heavy cream

Pastry:

- 4 cups of Kunāfah pastry
- 1 cup butter, melted

Garnish:

- ⅔ cup pistachios (chopped)

## Preparation

1. Start by preparing the syrup. You will need to boil the water, sugar and lemon juice together for 10 minutes. Afterward, remove the syrup from the stove and add the orange-blossom water. Allow it to cool down to room temperature before placing it in the fridge.
2. Now, make the filling. Form a smooth paste by combining the rice flour and some of the milk; you need to boil the remainder of the milk. Then add the rice flour paste, take it slow and mix constantly, you want there to be no lumps. Then turn the heat low. Cook for roughly 15-20 minutes or until the mixture thickens. Then add the sugar and stir. Allow the mixture to cool before you add the heavy cream.
3. Now spoon the melted butter onto the Kunāfah pastry. Be sure to coat each strand evenly.
4. Using a round, 12-inch pie pan spread half of the Kunāfah pastry onto the sides and the bottom of the pan. Then add the cream filling and place the other half of the pastry over the cream.
5. Bake for roughly 45 minutes on 350 degrees F (180 degrees C). Then bake for an additional 15 minutes on 425 degrees F (220 degrees C).
6. Remove from the oven and use a knife to loosen the sides of the pastry. Then turn out the Kunāfah onto a large plate. Drizzle the pastry with the sugar syrup and then sprinkle it with pistachios.

## Tips

Make sure that the syrup has cooled completely before drizzling it onto the Kunāfah.

## Tools

Pot, spoons, pie pan, sharp knife, plate

# Bosnian Börek

Ready in **60 minutes**

Serves **4 people**

**797 calories** per serving

## History

The story goes that if a woman in Bosnia can cook a good Börek then she is a good woman to marry. This dish is a proud part of Bosnian culture, despite its Turkish origins.

## Ingredients

- 4 cups of ground beef (preferably lean meat)
- 1 tablespoon of allspice (ground)
- 1 tablespoon of paprika
- Pinch of salt
- Black pepper
- 1 large potato (chopped)
- 1 large onion (chopped)
- 1 pack phyllo dough (roughly 16 ounces/450g)
- ¼ cup of melted butter

## Preparation

1. The first step is to preheat the oven to 400 degrees F (200 degrees C).
2. Use a large non-stick pan and brown the beef over a medium heat for roughly 5 to 8 minutes. Then drain the fat from the meat and add the paprika, the allspice, the salt, and the pepper. Put the beef into a large bowl and add the chopped potato and the chopped onion.
3. Unroll you phyllo pastry and place 2 sheets on a clean surface; stack them on top of one another. Now spoon about ⅛ th of the beef mixture along one long edge of the pastry. Then roll the pastry into a tube shape which encases the beef. Now shape the pastry tube into a coil. Transfer the coiled roll to an ungreased baking tray. Using a basting brush, brush the pastry with the melted butter. Repeat the process.
4. Bake the Börek for 20 -30 minutes until they are a nice golden brown color.

## Tips

To stop the Börek from uncoiling you need to pack them tightly together on the baking tray.

## Tools

Baking tray, basting brush, non-stick pan, bowl

# Mexican Conchas

Ready in **45 minutes**

Serves **16 people**

**339 calories** per serving

### History

Mexican Conchas date way back to the 18th Century when Mexico was colonized. The arrival of the French, Spanish and Italians meant different recipes were brought to the indigenous people of Mexico. The Concha was first invented by a group of nuns and indigenous woman. Concha means

### Ingredients

Dough:

- 2cups of flour (all purpose)
- ½ cup of sugar
- 1 ½ teaspoons of dry, active yeast
- ½ teaspoon of salt
- ½ cup of butter (unsalted at room temperature)
- 6 ½ tablespoons of egg
- 1 teaspoon of vanilla essence
- ½ cup of milk (warmed)

"shell" in Spanish. It is the national sweet bread of Mexico.

Topping:

- ½ cup of shortening
- ½ cup of icing sugar
- ½ cup of flour (all-purpose)
- 1 teaspoon of cinnamon

## Preparation

1. In an electric mixer, combine the flour, yeast, and sugar at a low-medium speed. Using the hook attachment add your butter and mix. Then add the eggs and vanilla essence. Slowly add the milk. Beat for 5-7 minutes at a low-medium speed. The dough should be quite soft and a little sticky.
2. Now transfer the dough on a lightly floured counter top and knead it gently while shaping it into a ball. Grease a large mixing bowl and place the dough ball inside. Cover the bowl with plastic wrap and a kitchen towel. Allow the dough to rest for two hours. The dough will double in size.
3. While the dough rises, make the topping. Cream your shortening and the icing sugar together. Slowly add the flour and then the cinnamon.
4. After two hours, place your dough back onto the floured counter and then divide it into balls (16 balls at 60g each). Place the balls onto your greased baking trays.
5. Now grease the top of each dough ball with some shortening. To add the topping, separate the paste into 16 little balls. Then use your hands to press down on each one to form a small, flat circle. Then place this small disk onto the ball of dough, and press it down firmly.
6. Use a Concha cutter or a knife to decorate them with the traditional shapes.
7. Leave the Conchas to rest in a warm place for 1 - 2 hours.
8. Place in a preheated oven at 325 degrees F (170 degrees C) for 20 minutes.

## Tips

Swap out the all-purpose flour for bread flour if you want a slightly softer texture.

## Tools

Rolling pin, mixing bowl, baking tray, sharp knife, measuring cups, Concha cutter, dough hook

# Canadian Butter Tart

Ready in **60 minutes**

Serves **12 people**

**529 calories** per serving

### History

Butter Tarts are considered by most people to be the classic Canadian dish however the invention of the Butter Tart dates back to before Canada even existed. Still, it is much loved by the Canadian people.

**Ingredients**

Pastry:

- 2 ¼ cups flour (all-purpose)
- 1 tablespoon of brown sugar
- ½ teaspoon of salt
- ½ cup of shortening (must be cold and cubed)
- ½ cup of butter (must be cold and cubed)
- 6 tablespoons of ice water

Filling:

- ½ cup of brown sugar
- ½ cup of corn syrup
- ¼ cup of butter (melted)
- 1 large egg
- 1 teaspoon of vanilla essence
- Pinch of Salt
- ½ cup of raisins

**Preparation**

1. In a large bowl, add the flour, salt and sugar. Then add the cold shortening and the cold butter. Blend together with your fingers until the butter and shortening are reduced to small pieces about the size of a pea.
2. Sprinkle the ice water over the surface. Using a fork, toss together until the water is worked into the mixture to form dough. Be careful not to overwork it.
3. Shape the dough into two pieces roughly 1-inch thick. Then wrap the dough in plastic wrap and allow it to rest in the fridge for 30 minutes.
4. After 30 minutes roll out the dough on a floured workspace. Cut the dough into rounds using a 4-inch cookie cutter. Place the rounds into muffin cups. Place in the fridge while preparing the filling.
5. Combine all of the filling ingredients with the exception of the raisins.
6. Then sprinkle enough raisins to form a single layer in the base of the pastry lined cups. Now fill about ⅔ of the cup with the syrup mixture.
7. Place in the oven and bake at 425 degrees F (220 degrees C) for about 12 - 15 minutes.
8. Allow the tarts to cool on a wire baking rack before removing them from the pans.

**Tips**

If you don't like raisins you can substitute them with chocolate chips, pecan nuts or walnuts

**Tools**

4-inch cookie cutter, large bowl, plastic wrap, muffin tray, wire baking rack

**RECIPE**

# British Scones

Ready in **60 minutes**

Serves **8 people**

**318 calories** per serving

### History

While Scones are believed to have originated in Scotland, there is nothing more British than tea and scones. They were first made using oats. Scones are classically served now with cream and jam.

**Ingredients**

Dough:

- 2 cups flour (all-purpose)
- ⅓ cup of sugar
- 1 teaspoon of baking powder
- ¼ teaspoon of baking soda
- Pinch of Salt
- 8 tablespoons butter (frozen and unsalted)
- ½ cup of buttermilk
- 1 egg

## Preparation

1. First, preheat your over to 400 degrees F (200 degrees C).
2. In a large bowl, combine the flour, ⅓ cup sugar, baking powder, baking soda and the salt. Use your grater to grate the butter into the flour. Then use your hands to work the butter into the flour mix.
3. In a separate bowl, whisk buttermilk and the egg.
4. Use a fork to add the wet ingredients to the dry ingredients. Then firmly push the dough into a ball.
5. Transfer to a lightly floured work surface. Form into an 8-inch circle which is roughly ¾-inch thick. Sprinkle the last 1 teaspoon of sugar. Use a knife to cut the dough into 8 triangles.
6. Line a baking tray with baking paper and place the scones an inch apart onto the tray. Bake for 15 minutes or until the scones are a golden brown.

## Tips

If you want round scones then use the top of a glass or a cookie cutter to cut the dough.

## Tools

Grater, bowls, knife, baking tray, baking paper

Printed in Great Britain
by Amazon

23469635R00048